A to Z

Poems for the Very Young

A to Z

Poems for the Very Young

by Julia Caroline Knowlton

Illustrations by Leah Owenby

Cover design by Shay Culligan
Cover art and design by Leah Owenby
Author and illustrator photo by Josh Cornwall

ISBN: 978-1-63980-624-9
Library of Congress Control Number: 2024942365

Kelsay Books
502 South 1040 East, A-119
American Fork, Utah 84003
Kelsaybooks.com

for

Claire Marguerite and Madeleine Marie

Contents

A

Amy flies on an airplane;
it disappears in the sky.
She sees both sun and rain
and counts clouds floating by.

B

Brett's sister is just a baby;
she can't even talk or walk.
When his sister is older, maybe
she'll draw with sidewalk chalk.

C

Claire hears a loud thunderclap
and sees lightning in the sky.
Her mom holds her on her lap
saying "soon this will all pass by."

D

Denise loves to dig in the dirt;
she plants potatoes and beans.
She gets dirt on her shirt
and her shoes and her favorite jeans.

E

Eve goes outside in the evening
to watch the sun set in the sky.
All the pink sunshine is leaving;
Eve sees one blue butterfly.

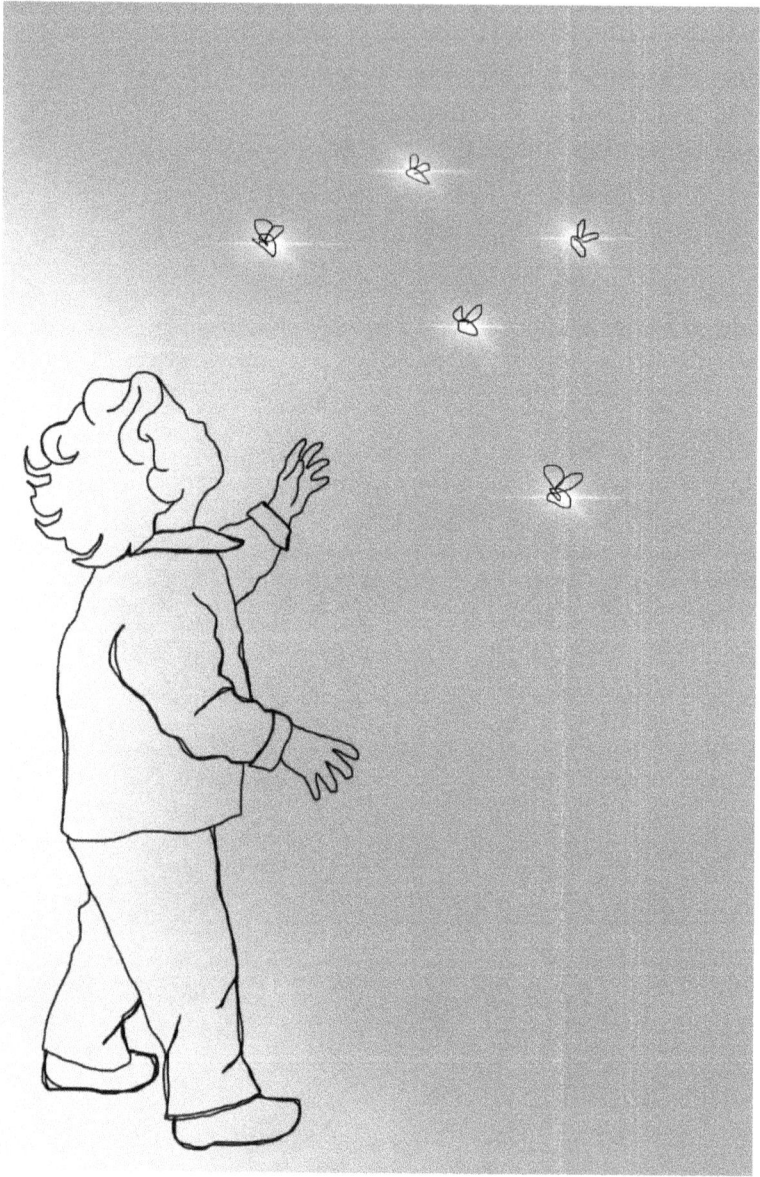

F

Frankie admires fireflies
floating in the warm summer night;
like magic lantern fairies,
they dance in golden flight.

G

Georgie sees a giant giraffe
eating the leaves of a tree.
It is covered with great big spots;
so much taller than you and me!

H

Henry has a speckled brown hen.
It lives in his backyard.
It lays eggs again and again;
nearby a rooster stands guard.

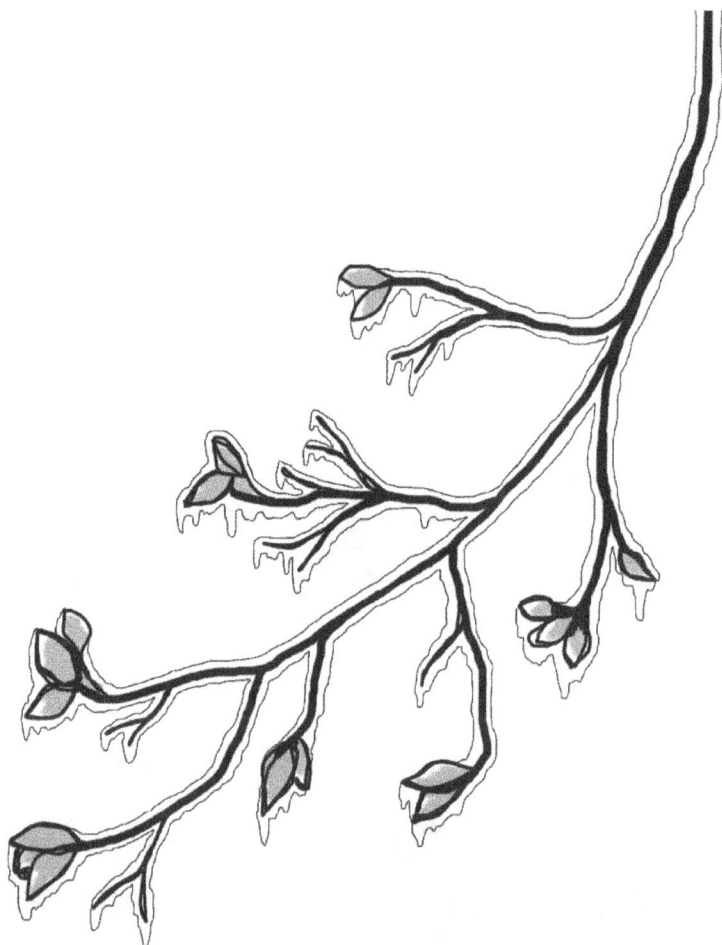

I

Ike's favorite season is winter.
He loves the snow and the ice.
His sister likes summer better
but for Ike, wintertime is nice.

J

Jake loves to run and jump
when he plays outside in the park.
He hops on rocks and tree stumps
and goes home before it gets dark.

K

Kay's grandma gives her a kiss
right on the top of her head.
"Sleep tight now, little miss,
let's get you snuggled in bed."

L

Lynn squeezes a yellow lemon;
she puts all the juice in a cup.
Then she pours in lots of sugar
and begins to stir it all up.

M

Maddie's kitty cat says *meow*
When it really wants to be fed.
If it already has enough food
then it meows for playtime instead.

N

Ned doesn't want to take a nap;
he wants to play with toys instead.
His mom holds him in her lap
and says, "Ned, it's time for bed."

O

Ollie went down to the ocean
to see blue waves and gold sand.
The seagulls and boats in motion
were far far away from the land.

P

Pia keeps toys in her pockets.
She has little cars and teddy bears.
Her favorite toy is a rocket;
she makes it soar in the air.

Q

Quinn dresses up like a queen;
she wears a golden crown.
Instead of wearing blue jeans
she wears a fancy purple gown.

R

Rosemary finds a red rose
growing along a stone wall.
She waters it with a garden hose
so it will grow nice and tall.

S

Stan loves to look at stars
shining silver in the dark night.
If he could keep them in a jar
he would have his own starlight.

T

Tracy has many nice toys;
she has puzzles and a doll.
Her little train brings her joy—
she likes it best of all.

U

Under a blue umbrella
Ursula walks on a rainy day.
She sees her friend Isabella;
together they go off to play.

V

Vicky made pretty valentines
and gave them to her mother.
Then she drew a pink heart
and gave it to her brother.

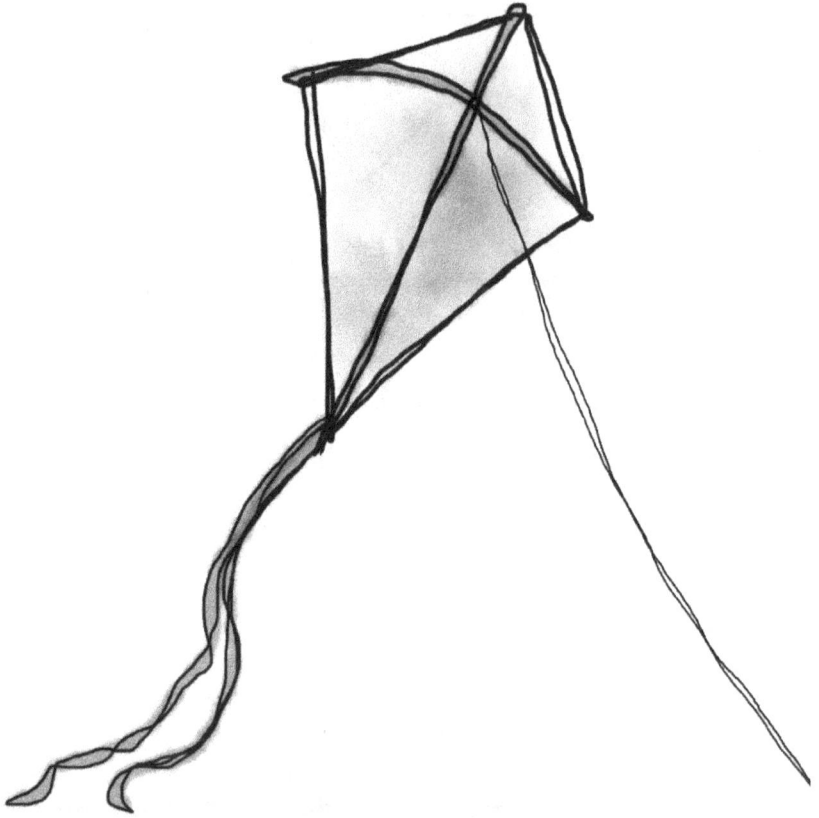

W

Wendy felt a cool wind
when she flew a yellow kite.
She and her brothers grinned
as the kite flew out of sight.

X

Tex found a cardboard box
and made it his hiding place.
He invited his orange toy fox
into his very own space.

Y

When Yolanda begins to yawn
she knows it is time to sleep.
She stays in bed until dawn
beneath the moonbeams so deep.

Z

Zachary takes a black crayon
and draws a zig and a zag.
He makes a fancy drawing on
the back of a white paper bag.

About the Author

Julia Caroline Knowlton is a poet, artist, and Professor of French at Agnes Scott College in Atlanta. She has published five books. Recognition for her poetry includes an Academy of American Poets College Prize and a 2018 Georgia Author of the Year award. She was a finalist for the 2022 Georgia Author of the Year award. This is her first book of poetry for children.

About the Illustrator

Leah Owenby is an Atlanta-based artist and aspiring gardener who lives with her favorite person and two ill-behaved but well-intentioned rescue dogs. She lives for connection and collaboration, the healing power of laughter, and a good story well told. Illustrating a book for children has been a lifelong dream and she's deeply grateful to Julia for bringing that dream to life.

Find her on Instagram:
@anxiousjester

www.ingramcontent.com/pod-product-compliance
Lightning Source LLC
Chambersburg PA
CBHW071113090426
42737CB00013B/2588